Presbyteries and Apostolic Teams

("Two are better than one;...")
Ecclesiastes 4:9

Presbyteries and Apostolic Teams

John Eckhardt

**("Two are better than one;...")
Ecclesiastes 4:9**

Crusaders Ministries
Chicago, Illinois

Presbyteries and Apostolic Teams
Published by:
Crusaders Ministries
P.O. Box 7211
Chicago, IL 60680
ISBN 1-883927-13-7

Editorial Consultant: Debra Marshall

Cover design and book production by:
DB & Associates Design Group, Inc.
dba Double Blessing Productions
P.O. Box 52756, Tulsa, OK 74152
www.doubleblessing.com

Printed in the United States of America.

Contents

The Church's Reproduction Cycle

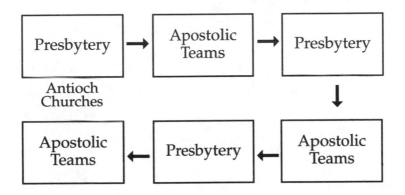

In his book, *The Normal Christian Church Life,* author Watchman Nee states:

> *"1. God establishes a church in a locality.*
>
> *2. He raises up gifted men in the church for the ministry.*
>
> *3. He sends some of these especially equipped men out into the work.*
>
> *4. These men establish churches in different places.*
>
> *5. God raises up other gifted men among these churches for the ministry of building them up.*
>
> *6. Some of these in turn are thrust forth to work in other fields.*
>
> *Thus, the work directly produces the churches, and the churches and the work progress, moving in an ever-recurring circle. The work always resulting directly in the founding of churches, and the churches always resulting indirectly in further work"* (pp. 183-184).

Introduction

There is no speech nor language, where their voice is not heard.

Their line is gone out through all the earth, and their words to the end of the world....

Psalm 19:3,4

The Harrison translation says, *"Their range extends throughout the earth."* This is a prophetic word concerning the reach of the Church. It is the will of God for our voice to be heard throughout the earth. The gospel will be preached through every speech and language in the world.

God is presently increasing the line of the church. The word *line* in the Hebrew is the word QAV meaning a cord for measuring. It represents a measure. A *measure* is the extent, dimensions, or quantity of something. The Church's line is its extension and outreach. The Church's line must go throughout the earth. This will affect all nations and tongues.

God's strategy for fulfilling this word is in presbyteries and apostolic teams. As we develop strong presbyteries and apostolic teams, we will see an increase in our measure and reach places we could not reach before.

Noted author Derek Prince states, *"Apostolic teams and presbyteries are two legs on which the Body of Christ move. If one leg is shorter than the other, the Body of Christ cannot function successfully."* Apostolic teams give the church the ability to expand beyond the local borders and touch the nations. Presbyteries enable the church to be governed properly, keeping the local assembly strong. Both are essential in helping the church fulfill its mission of impacting regions, territories, and nations.

A proper understanding of presbyteries and apostolic teams will help us to develop them and incorporate them into the local church. God is restoring both presbyteries and apostolic teams to the church. There is also a corresponding release of revelation concerning apostolic ministry. All around the world there is a hunger to walk in apostolic power and authority. This book is dedicated to help satisfy this hunger that is being birthed by the Holy Spirit.

I would like to thank Derek Prince for his teachings on this subject. I have also drawn from the books *Apostolic Strategies* by Jonathan David, and *The Complete Wineskin* by Harold Eberle. God is raising up men and women around the world to speak on these subjects. I pray that many more will grab hold of and begin to walk in these revelations to hasten the glorious return of our Lord and Savior Jesus Christ.

Presbyteries and Apostolic Teams

("Two are better than one;...")
Ecclesiastes 4:9

Chapter 1
Presbyteries

Neglect not the gift that is in thee, which was given thee by prophecy, with the laying on of the hands of the presbytery.

                                        1 Timothy 4:14

I will discuss presbyteries first because apostolic teams will be birthed out of strong presbyteries. An example of this is seen in the church at Antioch. The Antioch church is a model apostolic church that released teams to impact the world. From Antioch the apostles were released to plant churches all over the known world. The presbytery at Antioch consisted of prophets and teachers who ministered to the Lord and fasted. From this group Barnabas and Saul were chosen by the Holy Spirit and sent out to minister.

Let us first define the word presbytery. This word is only found one time in the New Testament in First Timothy 4:14. It is the Greek word *presbuterion* which means the order of elders. The presbytery is a group of elders that make up the government of the local church.

This verse gives us at least two characteristics of a presbytery. The *presbytery* should be able to minister prophetically, and they should be able to lay hands and impart. Timothy received a gift through the laying on of hands and prophecy. The presbytery is key to imparting and releasing strong ministry gifts.

A group of believers becomes a local church when government (elders) has been set in place. The setting and ordaining of elders is an apostolic function. As the apostles planted churches they also ordained elders (Acts 14:23). This is done through the apostolic team. Although the team is birthed from the presbytery, they in turn plant churches and raise up presbyteries. The result is a reproduction of presbyteries and teams with a continual expansion of the Kingdom of God.

The planting and building of New Testament churches is an <u>apostolic function.</u>

> *"Should a denomination plant churches? Again, this is commonly done, but to follow the New Testament pattern, it should be apostles who do the planting, and it should always be done relationally, not ecclesiastically. One hazard of planting churches denominationally is that it tends to produce uniformity — in part because decisions often are made by a central board who may function more like religious civil servants than a dynamic apostolic team"* (pg. 214).

> *Apostles Today*
> Barney Coombs

It takes a pioneering, breakthrough anointing to penetrate into new regions and establish churches. Ordaining and setting elders is necessary to establish the government of the local church. Without proper government the church will not be able to withstand the attacks of darkness and remain strong.

Apostles and apostolic teams have grace to identify and set in place the leaders of the local assembly. Apostles and prophets are anointed to release gifted individuals into leadership. Churches that are set up through the apostolic anointing become strong local assemblies that impact the regions they are called to.

Although the books of Timothy and Titus are often called *pastoral epistles,* they are in reality *apostolic.* Both Timothy and Titus were apostles. They were both a part of Paul's apostolic team and Timothy is specifically identified as an apostle in First Thessalonians 2:6. Paul is giving them the qualifications of overseers. Timothy and Titus functioned apostolically to set elders in place in the local churches.

> **To Titus, mine own after the common faith: Grace, mercy, and peace, from God the Father and the Lord Jesus Christ our Savior.**
>
> **For this cause left I thee in Crete, that thou shouldest set in order the things that are wanting, and ordain elders in every city, as I had appointed thee:...**
>
> **For a BISHOP must be blameless, as the steward of God; not selfwilled, not soon angry, not given to wine, no striker, not given to filthy lucre.**
>
> **Titus 1:4,5,7**

Here we see that elders are bishops (overseers) in the local church. They are chosen based on their leadership and character. Those chosen and ordained will become the presbytery of the local church.

The formation of presbyteries is important because this group will help determine the direction and success of the local church. Presbyteries can be formed initially and over a period of time. They must never be formed presumptuously. Here are some important points to remember when forming presbyteries:

1. It should be done with apostolic wisdom (Titus 1:5).
2. It should be done in humility with fasting (Acts 14:23).
3. It should be done with prayer (Luke 6:12,13).
4. It should be done by the direction of the Holy Spirit (Acts 13:2).

To attempt the presbytery formation any other way is to invite disaster. It will not work if done with fleshly wisdom. It only works by the grace of God. This is why it must be done apostolically. Apostles (sent ones) must rely on the grace of God (1 Corinthians 15:10).

When the elders gather together on a regular basis, seeking the Lord and ministering unto Him, they can expect to receive God's direction for the local church (Acts 13:1). God releases His purposes and divine strategies through the presbytery. A part of this strategy will be the release of apostolic teams.

The presbytery becomes the governmental authority of the local church. Jonathan David states in <u>Apostolic Strategies,</u>

"Paul raised up men in the local bases to be elders so that each church had self-government and autonomy. He established proper leadership structure for each of these churches so that they become responsible for their own growth and spiritual well-being. Each church raised up through the Antioch missions was responsible for its own growth, mission and development of ministries."

Derek Prince states:

"On the earthly level, there is no human authority over presbyteries and apostolic teams. Jesus governs

4

these direct from heaven through the Holy Spirit (Acts 13:1-4; 16:6-10). Historically man has set other individuals or groups over presbyteries and apostolic teams, and frustrated the government of Jesus. The usual result is some form of bureaucracy, but this does not meet the real needs. Israel found it difficult to live under God's invisible government and asked for a human king (see 1 Samuel 8:4-22). In such a case, visible human government tends to come between the Lord and His people, and to drain the resources of the people" (Apostolic Teams — tape series).

The presbytery should therefore be an autonomous governing body of the local church, led by the Lord Jesus through the Holy Spirit.

And God has set some in the church, first apostles, secondarily prophets, thirdly teachers, after that miracles, then gifts of healings, helps, governments, diversities of tongues.
1 Corinthians 12:28

"We also should note that the first three gifts — apostle, prophet, and teacher — stand out in a distinct manner. In other Bible passages we see these three gifts specifically being named among the church leadership. Christians with gifts of miracles, healings, helps, administration, and tongues may or may not be part of the presbytery. The three highest gifts definitely are among the presbytery.

"In First Corinthians 12:11-28, we are told that the Holy Spirit places us in the Body where He chooses, and that He has chosen to place apostles first, prophets second, teachers third, and so on. This is the pattern of authority evident in the Early Church" (pg. 63).

The Complete Wineskin
Harold Eberle

5

A *presbytery* is a group of elders that comprise the government of the local church. The highest ranking ministry gifts of the church are apostles, prophets and teachers. These gifts when present in presbytery serve as co-elders. There should be a mutual respect for the authority and rankings within the presbytery. A team of apostles, prophets and teachers carry a tremendous amount of authority in the spirit realm. These are the governmental anointings of the church. The Holy Spirit will work through this authority as they yield themselves to him for guidance and direction.

The presbytery is stationary and shepherds the flock of God. The apostolic and prophetic anointings are necessary to keep the local church updated in revelation and spiritual technologies. The apostolic anointing is important because it is a pioneering and progressive anointing. These anointings help keep the church on the cutting edge. The teaching anointing helps keep the church grounded in the Word of God. The presbytery is responsible for doctrine and rulership. They will labor in the word and doctrine (1 Timothy 5:17).

The three highest governmental gifts in the Church are apostles, prophets and teachers. The different anointings and rankings in the church should be taught and understood by the saints, especially the leadership. The "set man" (Numbers 27:16) will usually be an apostle who is recognized and respected by the other members of the presbytery. All members of the presbytery will not have equal rank. God does not operate through a system of democracy (See diagram on following page).

6

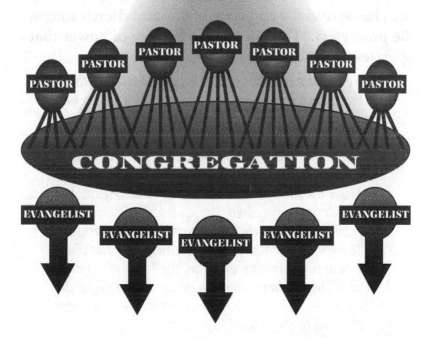

On the other hand, God does not rule through dictators. The "set man" needs to recognize the other ministry gifts and their corresponding authority. Prophets and teachers also operate in tremendous authority. Kings, who were Old Testament types of apostles, got into trouble when they did not recognize and respect the other anointings (prophets and priests). The key is mutual respect and a proper understanding of spiritual ranking. Remember apostolic ministry is essentially team ministry. It is dangerous to put full authority in the hands of one man. Few men can handle it. God in His wisdom has spread the authority of the local church among the presbytery. This provides a balance of power that operates by the grace of God.

> *"No one likes the thought of being led by a dictator, and that is not what the Bible teaches. But neither do the Scriptures support the democratic model for church government. The pattern that we see in the pages of the New Testament is one of collective leadership, where maximum room is given for discussion, dialogue and input, but the final decision rests with leadership. We see this demonstrated in the Council of Jerusalem (Acts 15) where much discussion and consultation (not to mention heated debate) ensued over the place of the law and circumcision in the lives of Gentile believers. In the end, James stood up and brought the judgment — with which they all agreed — and peace was restored to the church" (pg. 99).*

Apostles Today
Barney Coombs

This is not intended to undermine the authority of a strong apostle. Apostles have strong anointings and walk in tremendous power and authority. There is nothing wrong with strong leaders. Apostles by nature are strong in vision and ability. Apostolic leaders should not be controlled by carnal elders. This is why presbyteries must be put in place by the Holy Spirit's wisdom, and not fleshly wisdom.

Sometimes the elders appointed by a leader are only "yes men". They should not be appointed because they are "yes men", but rather because they are chosen and anointed by God. The apostle, when in the local church, will be a co-elder (1 Peter 5:1). The elders within a presbytery will be in covenant relationship, with mutual respect and love resulting in the unity of the Spirit. Jonathan David states, *"Often the hierarchy of pyramidal type of leadership structure provides a good control of the church but retards the growth of the church in its creativity and inner dynamics. The apostolic structure is a wheel within a wheel. The man in the front should be apostolic and he must be surrounded by a team."*

The traditional concept of a pastor over a church with associates and assistants is being challenged by a revelation of presbytery. Terms such as *associate* and *assistant* are not scriptural. We need to use Holy Spirit words to understand His anointings (1 Corinthians 2:12,13).

Harold Eberle states, *"Since we can find no example in the New Testament of a pastor leading a local church or participating among the presbytery of a church, where does the pastor fit in? And why did God not list the gift of pastor among the authority gifts in First Corinthians 12:28? God's intention was that pastors work among the sheep, not rule over the local church. As the evangelist is to be among the unsaved, the pastor must be among the congregation. The pastor's primary role is that of gathering in the sheep."*

The pastoral gifting is designed by God to touch the sheep in an intimate way. Many local churches have hundreds of pastors sitting in the pews that need to be recognized and released into their ministries. The church may use the terms "cell leaders" or "care leaders", but God calls them "pastors" (Ephesians 4:11).

We have traditionally called the leaders of local churches "pastors". This is a result of the unbelief in the larger segment of the church in apostles and prophets for today. With the restoration of apostles and prophets, we must redefine the gifts and rediscover where they fit in and belong in the church.

Graham Cooke states:

"Examine the whole principle of one-man ministry in the church. A cursory look at the Scriptures tells us that the term pastor is not a descriptive word for a local church leader. It is only used once in connection with the five fold ministries of apostle, prophet, pastor, teacher, and evangelist (see Ephesians 4:11). The correct term for local leadership is the plural of elder to denote a team ministry (Read Acts 11:30; 14:23; 15:2-4,6,22; 16:4, 20:17,28; First Timothy 3:1-7. 5:17, Titus 1:5-9; James 5:14, and First Peter 5:1-4.

In all the New Testament churches established under apostolic and prophetic input we read of elders (plural) being appointed in every city (See Acts 14:23). The apostolic team working through and in support of local teams of elders would train, equip, empower, and release the people to do the work of the ministry. The fivefold ministries are consultant gifts to the church leaders (and often are leaders in churches themselves) to enable them to be built wisley into the place of anointed significance that God desires for them in that locality. What we have in thousands of churches today is a one-man ministry approach that cannot be defended in scripture" (pp.43-44).

> *"As we understand it, the role of pastor does not solely relate to local church government; it is a consultant gift belonging to the fivefold ministries (see Ephesians 4:11-13). Scripture is clear in its outline that elders have a close working relationship with apostolic ministry (see Acts 15; 16:4; 20:17; 21:18). They are appointed by apostles (see Acts 14:23, Titis 1:5-11) who lay down guidelines for behavior in ministry and who express certain qualities required to hold this particular office in the local church (see First Thessalonians 5:12,13, First Timothy 3:1-7; 5:17-20, Titus 1:5-11, James 5:14,15, First Peter 5:1-4)"* (pg. 87).

A Divine Confrontation
Graham Cooke

God is presently speaking to many pastors (leaders of local churches) to embrace and begin to walk in an apostolic call. There is a transition taking place across the earth. Many leaders are transitioning from pastoral functions to apostolic functions. Many leaders are beginning to understand their true callings once the limitations of religion and tradition are broken.

Apostles should be a part of the presbytery if they are stationary; and leaders in an apostolic team, if they are mobile. The presbytery has the grace to lay hands on ministers and prophesy (1 Timothy 4:14). The result will be a release of spiritual gifts. Apostolic teams can be released in this way through the presbytery. The formation of strong presbyteries is essential to release apostolic teams. *"Until apostolic teams become functional, the Church should consider itself in a process of ongoing development"* (Derek Prince, *Apostolic Teams* — tape series).

Ordination

And he goeth up into a mountain, and calleth unto him whom he would: and they came unto him.

> And he ordained twelve, that they should be with him, and that he might send them forth to preach,
>
> And to have power to heal sicknesses, and to cast out devils.
>
> **Mark 3:13-15**

Jesus is the perfect apostle (sent one). One of the first things he did was gather together a team. The twelve were ordained to be with Jesus. They became a part of his team. To *ordain* means to set, place or appoint. They were appointed by the Lord to be apostles (sent ones). Jesus also gave them power to heal sicknesses and to cast out devils. There was an authority released at the point of ordination.

> And when they had ORDAINED them elders in every city, and had prayed with fasting, they commanded them to the Lord, on whom they believed.
>
> **Acts 14:23**

Presbyteries consist of ordained elders who are responsible to govern the local church. Ordination is an apostolic functions that sets qualified leaders into positions of authority that is recognized in the spirit realm. Ordination should be accompanied by the laying on of hands and prophecy (1 Timothy 4:14). There is a release of spiritual power in ordination. The recipient receives an impartation that equips them to function in their ordained office.

> Ye have not chosen me, but I have chosen you, and ORDAINED you, that ye should go and bring forth fruit, and that your fruit should remain; that whatsoever ye shall ask the Father in my name, he may give it you.
>
> **John 15:16**

Fruitfulness should be the result of ordination. If ordination is carried out properly, we will see the release of abundant and fruitful ministries. Ordained ministers will bring forth fruit that remains. Our churches will have lasting fruit if presbyteries are raised up and set properly.

Honor

And the Lord said unto Moses, Take thee Joshua the son of Nun, a man in whom is the spirit, and lay thine hand upon him;

And set him before Eleazar the priest, and before all the congregation; and give him a charge in their sight.

And thou shalt put some of thine honour upon him, that all the congregation of the children of Israel may be obedient.

Numbers 27:18-20

Moses was commanded to lay his hands upon Joshua and place honor upon him. This was to be done before the entire congregation. When leaders are ordained publicly, honor is placed upon them. There is a transfer of honor through the laying on of hands. The congregation will then honor them and become obedient.

Joshua was honored by Moses and prepared to assume the mantle of leadership. It is an honor to be ordained. We are warned not to lay hands suddenly upon any man (1 Timothy 5:22). This is in reference to ordination. We are to be careful who we place honor upon. *Honor* means high public esteem, fame and glory. This is what is released through ordination.

Many desire ordination for this purpose only. The motive should not be self-promotion or fame. One of the qualifications of a bishop is NOT SELF-WILLED (Titus 1:7). Selfishness has no place in a presbytery. Self-promoting people should not become a part of a team. Moses was told specifically whom to lay his hands upon.

Joshua had the right spirit, and was able to receive honor. Everyone cannot handle honor (Proverbs 26:1).

> **And the Lord said unto Moses, Gather unto me seventy men of the elders of Israel, whom thou knowest to be the elders of the people, and officers over them; and bring them unto the tabernacle of the congregation, that they may stand there with thee.**
>
> **And I will come down and talk with thee there: and I will take of the spirit which is upon thee, and will put it upon them; and they shall bear the burden of the people with thee, that thou bear it not thyself alone.**
>
> **Numbers 11:16,17**

The principle of eldership runs throughout the Word of God. We even find in the book of Revelation elders worshiping before the throne (Revelation 4:4,10). Moses (a type of an apostle) was told to gather seventy elders for the purpose of helping him govern the people. A portion of Moses' spirit would be placed upon the seventy.

A presbytery can be apostolic if there are apostles present. An apostolic spirit can rest upon each member of the presbytery if the "set man" is an apostle. This means each member of the presbytery can walk in an apostolic dimension although all will not be apostles. A presbytery will have apostolic prophets and apostolic teachers. The elders will have an apostolic vision and will walk in apostolic power and grace.

God is raising up apostolic presbyteries around the globe. We are seeing groups of elders operate in power to impact the regions and territories where they are sent. These groups have a pioneering and breakthrough anointing to penetrate into the spirit realm and cause the heavens to be opened over their cities and nations. This causes great blessing to be released in the given area. Signs, wonders, healings, deliverances, and salvation will result. The presbytery becomes an instrument in the hands of the Lord to effect change and bring revival.

The result will be apostolic, governing churches that will influence and impact cities, regions, territories and nations. We call these churches "Antioch churches". *Apostolic Strategies* author, Jonathan David, states:

"When a whole church takes upon itself an apostolic burden to reach their regions and beyond, a new break-through of apostolic endeavor is on the horizon."

The church at Antioch responded to the call of God and took upon itself the burden to release teams and affect nations. Antioch became a regional base through which the Holy Spirit initiated apostolic outreach across the nations. Antioch is our model apostolic church. Next, we will look at the other "leg" of the church — APOSTOLIC TEAMS.

Chapter 2
Antioch Churches:
The Development and
Release of Apostolic Teams

Now there were in the church that was at Antioch
certain prophets and teachers; as Barnabas, and
Simeon that was called Niger, and Lucius of Cyrene,
and Manaen, which had been brought up with Herod
the tetrarch, and Saul.

As they ministered to the Lord, and fasted, the
Holy Ghost said, Separate me Barnabas and Saul for
the work whereunto I have called them.

And when they had fasted and prayed, and laid
hands on them, they sent them away.

Acts 13:1-3

*"The church in Antioch is the model church shown us
in God's Word because it was the first to come into being
after the founding of the churches connected with the Jews
and the Gentiles. In Acts chapter two we see the church
in connection with the Jews established in Jerusalem, and
in chapter ten we see the church in connection with the
Gentiles established in the house of Cornelius. It was just
after the establishment of these churches that the church
in Antioch from the very outset stood on absolutely clear
church ground. It is of no little significance that the disciples were first called Christians in Antioch (Acts 11:26).*

17

It was there that the peculiar characteristics of the Christian and the Christian church were first clearly manifested, for this reason it may be regarded as the pattern church for this dispensation" (pg. 19).

The Normal Christian
Church Life
Watchman Nee

We define an *Antioch Church* as an apostolic, governmental church that impacts regions and territories. These churches are spiritual hubs. They are strategic churches raised up by God to initiate apostolic endeavors across the earth.

Antioch churches provide an atmosphere for the development and release of apostolic teams. *Apostolic teams* consist of apostles with other five-fold ministry giftings who are able to go into a region and build apostolically. Apostles will lead the team and draw from the other anointings (especially prophets) to breakthrough in churches and territories to which they have been sent. The team preaches, teaches, prophesies and operates in the gifts of the Holy Spirit. They will also minister deliverance and healing. The apostolic team is a part of God's strategy to release the plan and purposes of God throughout the earth.

The apostolic team imparts a fresh spirit measure into the churches and regions they visit. They release new revelation and present truth to the believers. The team ignites new moves of the Holy Spirit and bring upgrades in spiritual technologies. <u>One of God's end-time strategies is the release of apostolic teams.</u> (The apostolic team does not come to duplicate what the local leadership has already produced, rather to release a new Spirit measure into the church.)

There is a Macedonian call throughout the earth for the apostolic team. Many churches and regions need the help of these teams. <u>Local churches and regions would do well to bring in an apostolic team.</u> <u>The *apostolic team* will bring blessing, refreshing, revelation and impartation.</u>

The apostolic team is a way of connecting governing apostolic churches to different churches, regions, and nations. The spiritual deposit and resources that exist in the apostolic church can be distributed throughout the nations through apostolic teams. The local church can have more than one apostolic team. This can be done by recognizing other apostolic leaders within the church (or network) and releasing them to head teams that are sent out. In this way, the local church can affect many regions and nations.

The apostolic team is important because no apostle can do all the work required of apostolic ministry alone. Jonathan David states, *"to meet the intensity of his own burden to build strong local churches an apostle knows that raising up an apostolic team of builders alongside him is not only necessary but vital to have ministry success."*

The apostle attracts and releases other five-fold ministers. This is one of the most important functions of apostolic ministry. Teams can breakthrough where individuals cannot. Apostles and prophets working together make a formidable team in the spirit.

The First Team

The first team released from Antioch consisted of Barnabas and Saul. They also took with them John Mark (Acts 13:5). This group gives us a picture of what is needed within a team. We know that both Barnabas and Saul flowed prophetically because they are identified as prophets in Acts 13:1. Barnabas' name means the son of consolation (Acts 4:36). Barnabas was an encourager. He came to Antioch and exhorted the new church to cleave unto the Lord (Acts 11:22,23). This is important because one of the main functions of the apostolic team is to encourage and comfort. Barnabas-type apostles and prophets are needed on the apostolic team.

Saul was a man well-versed in the Scriptures. He was an apostle of revelation. He was focused and entirely sold out concerning his commission. He was able to teach and preach because of his diligent study of the Word. This is important because the apostolic team must be able to bring new revelation and teaching of the Word. They must upgrade churches and regions with new insights from heaven. We need Paul-type apostles and prophets on the team that are skillful in the Word and able to impart truth to believers.

John Mark was a young man who turned back on the first journey. There is no detail given concerning why he returned before the first journey was complete. We can only speculate that he was not willing or able at this time to handle the rigors of apostolic ministry. This eventually caused a separation between Barnabas and Paul. Barnabas wanted to take him on the second trip, but Paul refused. Evidently, Barnabas' encouraging nature would not let him give up on John Mark (Acts 15:37-41). Mark consequently matured because Paul later calls for him while in prison (2 Timothy 4:11).

Mark represents an understudy apostle. It is good to have those on the team who are being trained and mentored. We must not neglect young people who have callings and destinies that need to be released. We now have the gospel of Mark because of Barnabas' encouragement.

The Second Team

The second team consisted of Paul and Silas. We have already mentioned Paul's characteristics. Silas is called a prophet in Acts 15:32. He was an exhorter and helped confirm the churches. He is referred to as one of the "chief men among the brethren" (Acts 15:22). He is referred to as an apostle (1 Thessalonians 1:1 and 2:6,7). He was not a novice, but recognized as a leader in the Jerusalem church. He is a prophetic apostle who labored on the apostolic team to confirm and strengthen the churches.

Timothy also became a part of this team. He is referred to as a faithful son in the ministry by Paul. He was taught the Scriptures from an early age (2 Timothy 3:15). He is another example of an understudy apostle. Paul told him to let no man despise his youth (1 Timothy 4:12). This shows us the importance of having young people on the apostolic team.

Timothy was not self-seeking (Philippians 2:19-21). Members of the apostolic team should not use the team as a means of promoting their own ministries. People who are self-seeking and have worldly ambition should not be part of an apostolic team.

Other Team Members

Other team members include Titus, Epaphroditus, Sopater, Aristarchus, Secundus, Gaius, Tychicus and Trophimus (2 Corinthians 12:18; Philippians 2:25; Acts 20:4). Titus was left in Crete to ordain elders and set things in order (Titus 1:5). These are both apostolic functions. Titus was evidently a man who could operate in biblical order and authority. He was able to handle responsibility. Team members must be responsible and trustworthy.

Epaphroditus was a hard worker, a fighter, and one that ministered to Paul's wants (Philippians 2:25). He had a servant's heart. Apostolic team members should have servants hearts. They should also have a soldier's mentality. They must be able to endure hardness.

One of the signs of a true apostle is the ability to gather other ministry gifts for training, activation and release. This was a characteristic of Paul's ministry. The following scriptures give us a picture of the many people associated with his team.

> **So he sent into Macedonia two of them that ministered unto him, Timotheus and Erastus; but he himself stayed in Asia for a season.**
>
> **And the whole city was filled with confusion: and having caught Gaius and Aristarchus, men of Macedonia, Paul's companions in travel, they rushed with one accord into the theatre.**
>
>

Acts 19:22,29

> **Timotheus my workfellow, and Lucius, and Jason, and Sosipater, my kinsmen, salute you.**
>
> **I Tertius, who wrote this epistle, salute you in the Lord.**
>
> **Gaius mine host, and of the whole church, saluteth you. Eratus the chamberlain of the city saluteth you, and Quartus a brother.**
>
>

Romans 16:21-23

Roger Sapp, author of *The Last Apostles On Earth*, states:

> *"Whenever you find this ministry, you should find individuals like Timothy and others whom God is discipling in ministry by means of the apostle. The apostle will always have individuals God has given him to train. He will have young prophets, teachers, evangelists, and pastors to encourage and prepare for greater ministry than his own. God will call some of them into apostolic ministry as well."*

The apostolic team is a practical way of training ministers through hands-on ministry. The apostle has a grace to train and release ministries quickly.

In addition to those being trained, mature elders should be released from the presbytery to be a part of the team. This will make room for others in the local church to rise up and fill in the vacancies. The result will be the continual development of strong ministry gifts within the local church and a continual release of qualified leaders to be a part of apostolic teams. This will break stagnation in the local church that results when there is no release of apostolic teams.

The following are principles gleaned from the word of God concerning apostolic teams. Many of them are taken from Paul's first letter to the Thessalonians:

1. THE MISSION OF THE APOSTOLIC TEAM: The Apostolic team brings salvation to the ends of the earth.

> **For so hath the Lord commanded us, saying, I have set thee to be a light of the Gentiles, that thou shouldest be for salvation unto the ends of the earth.**
>
> **Acts 13:47**

Jonathan David, author of *Apostolic Strategies Affecting Nations*, calls the apostolic team *"God's strategic plan to reach the nations."* Acts 13:47 is a quote from Isaiah 49:6. Paul saw the apostolic ministry as one that brings salvation to the ends of the earth. Antioch churches will release apostolic teams to the nations. They will bring deliverance to many regions beyond the local church. The apostolic team brings light and revelation to regions of spiritual darkness and ignorance. The apostolic team is sent by the command of God. This means they are sent with the authority of heaven. Their authority is recognized by the spirit realm in the regions where they are sent.

2. *THE NEED FOR THE APOSTOLIC TEAM:* The Apostolic team confirms and exhorts believers in the local churches — especially in places where the church is persecuted.

And when they had preached the gospel to that city, and had taught many, they returned again to Lystra, and to Iconium, and Antioch.

Confirming the souls of the disciples, and exhorting them to continue in the faith, and that we must through much tribulation enter into the kingdom of God.

Acts 14:21,22

Apostolic teams are especially needed in nations where the church suffers persecution. They will confirm these churches and exhort them. To *confirm* means to strengthen. It is important to strengthen churches that have suffered, that they may be able to continue their witness. God will use Antioch churches to strengthen other churches that live in difficult regions of the world. The visit of the apostolic team will help believers continue in the faith.

3. *THE AUTHORITY OF THE APOSTOLIC TEAM:* The Apostolic team can ordain elders in the churches they plant and establish.

And when they had ordained them elders in every church, and had prayed with fasting, they commended them to the Lord, on whom they believed.

Acts 14:23

This is the beginning of the reproduction of presbyteries and apostolic teams. Once a new presbytery has been established in a region, they are responsible to seek the Lord and eventually release apostolic teams. God is a God of multiplication and increase. These are proven strategies to impact regions and fulfill the Great Commission.

4. *THE DECREES OF THE APOSTOLIC TEAM:* The Apostolic team delivers Apostolic decrees and keeps the local churches operating in the liberty of the spirit.

And as they went through the cities, they delivered them the decrees for to keep, that were ordained of the apostles and elders which were at Jerusalem.

Acts 16:4

The first doctrinal controversy in the church was concerning the law. Some Jewish believers were teaching that the Gentiles had to be circumcised and keep the law of Moses. The church convened in Jerusalem to resolve the issue. They issued a decree to the Gentile churches that freed them from the requirement of circumcision and the law. A team was sent to deliver the decree.

The issue was liberty. Satan always attempts to stop the liberty of the local churches. Apostolic teams help the local churches maintain the liberty of the Holy Spirit. They break off man made restrictions and rules that hinder the church. Apostolic ministry releases liberty (2 Corinthians 3:17).

5. *THE STRENGTH OF THE APOSTOLIC TEAM:* The Apostolic team helps the local churches become established in the faith and helps the local churches to grow.

And so were the churches established in the faith, and increased in number daily.

Acts 16:5

The apostolic team helps establish the believers of the local church. To *establish* means to make secure, stable or permanent. The church must be established in order to be strong.

Once churches are established they are put in a position for growth. Apostolic ministry is necessary to the health and vitality of the church. The apostolic teams releases an anointing for church growth. Churches become stronger and healthier after the visit of the apostolic team.

6. *THE LEADING OF THE APOSTOLIC TEAM:* The Apostolic team must be led by the Holy Spirit.

Now when they had gone throughout Phrygia and the region of Galatia, and were forbidden of the Holy Ghost to preach the word in Asia,

Acts 16:6

There may be places where the team is forbidden to go. Jesus governs the team through the Holy Spirit. He is the One directing and leading the team. This is what makes the team successful. They depend upon the leading of the Holy Spirit.

Apostolic teams must not be presumptuous. They cannot operate in fleshly wisdom, but are entirely dependent upon the Holy Spirit. New territories must be approached only by the Lord's direction. To go any other way is to invite disaster or failure.

7. *THE CALL FOR THE APOSTOLIC TEAM:* The Apostolic team responds to the call of regions that need help.

AND a vision appeared to Paul in the night; There stood a man of Macedonia, and prayed him, saying, Come over into Macedonia, and help us.

And after he had seen the vision, immediately we endeavored to go into Macedonia, assuredly gathering that the Lord had called us for to go preach the gospel unto them.

Acts 16:9,10

Antioch churches will respond to the Macedonian call of churches in need of help. The apostolic team is anointed by God to help. It is the nature and desire of the apostolic team to help build up churches. There is a Macedonian call being sent through the earth for apostolic teams to come and help.

As we build apostolic teams, we will be in a position to respond to this call for help.

8. THE POWER OF THE APOSTOLIC TEAM: The Apostolic team breaks the power of python.

AND it came to pass, as we went to prayer, a certain damsel possessed with a spirit of divination met us, which brought her masters much gain by soothsaying:

The same followed Paul and us, and cried, saying, These men are the servants of the most high God, which shew unto us the way of salvation.

And this did she many days. But Paul, being grieved, turned and said to the spirit, I command thee in the name of Jesus Christ to come out of her. And he came out the same hour.   **Acts 16:16-18**

The spirit of divination is the spirit of PYTHON. *Python is a constrictor.* This spirit will slowly choke the life out of the church. Pythons kill their victims by squeezing the breath out of them. This is the only detailed apostolic deliverance given in the Bible.

When python's power is broken, there will be a greater liberty in the church. The church will be able to breath again.

The apostolic team will help destroy the spirit of witchcraft. Churches that are in regions where there is strong witchcraft will benefit from the visit of the apostolic team. Believers in the local churches will receive deliverance from witchcraft spirits and generational curses. This will release them to flow in the gifts and operations of the Holy Spirit.

27

9. THE ENTRANCE OF THE APOSTOLIC TEAM: The Apostolic team has an entrance provided by the Lord.

> For yourselves, brethren, know our entrance in unto you, that it was not in vain.
>
> 1 Thessalonians 2:1

God opens the door for the apostolic team. We should pray for great and effectual doors to be opened (1 Corinthians 16:9). God will set before us open doors that no man can shut (Revelation 3:8). When the door is opened and the people respond, the entrance is not in vain. The apostolic team should expect great results.

10. THE BOLDNESS OF THE APOSTOLIC TEAM: The Apostolic team ministers in boldness.

> But even after that we had suffered before, and were shamefully entreated, as ye know, at Philippi, we were bold in our God to speak unto you the gospel of God with much contention.
>
> 1 Thessalonians 2:2

Boldness is a characteristic of the apostolic ministry. Team members need to operate in boldness and not be intimidated by opposition or persecution. Paul and his team were bold in Thessalonica in spite of being jailed previously in Phillipi. The attacks of darkness should not stop the apostolic team.

11. THE PURITY OF THE APOSTOLIC TEAM: The Apostolic team has pure motives.

> For our exhortation was not of deceit, nor of uncleanness, nor in guile.
>
> 1 Thessalonians 2:3

The apostolic team does not operate in deceit or deception. They speak the truth with pure hearts. They do not come to mislead. People on the apostolic team must have pure motives. False apostles and prophets

28

operate in deceit, especially in the area of finances. True apostles and prophets are driven by a commission, not financial gain. They have no ulterior motives.

12. THE TRUST OF THE APOSTOLIC TEAM: The Apostolic team's desire is to please God.

> **But as we were allowed of God to be put in trust with the gospel, even so we speak; not as pleasing men, but God, which trieth our hearts.**
>
> **1 Thessalonians 2:4**

The apostolic team has been put in trust with a message. The team cannot violate this trust. They must be faithful to preach and release the revelation committed to them by God. This is an awesome responsibility, and the team will one day be judged based on this trust.

Pleasing God is the motivation of the apostolic team. The team does not have a man pleasing spirit. Many religious groups have a desire to please men. This is not the case with the apostolic team. Sometimes their message may be controversial or offensive in the eyes of men.

13. THE MOTIVE OF THE APOSTOLIC TEAM: The Apostolic team does not minister for financial gain.

> **For neither at any time used we flattering words, as ye know, nor a cloke of covetousness; God is witness:**
>
> **1 Thessalonians 2:5**

The ministry is not a cloak of covetousness for the apostolic team. They do not preach messages for financial gain. Covetous people should not be a part of an apostolic team. Financial gain is not the motive of the team. They go because they "ARE SENT". Sent ones are driven by a commission, not money.

14. THE HUMILITY OF THE APOSTOLIC TEAM: The Apostolic team should never be a burden to the local church.

> Nor of men sought we glory, neither of you, nor
> yet of others, when we might have been burdensome,
> as the apostles of Christ.
>
> 1 Thessalonians 2:6

The apostolic team must never become a financial burden to the local churches. This does not mean that the local churches should not bless the team financially. There are, however, places where the apostolic team will go that cannot afford to bring an entire team. This is especially true of poor regions.

The members of an apostolic team can support themselves if necessary (1 Thessalonians 2:9).

15. THE GENTLENESS OF THE APOSTOLIC TEAM: The Apostolic team ministers in gentleness.

> But we were gentle among you, even as a nurse
> cherisheth her children:
>
> 1 Thessalonians 2:7

The team will not be "hard" on the church. They minister with care and compassion. They do not come to "beat" the sheep, but to "bless" the sheep. The team ministers by the meekness and gentleness of Christ (2 Corinthians 10:1). Sent ones are not harsh and dictatorial. False apostles will smite you on the face (2 Corinthians 11:20).

16. THE IMPARTATION OF THE APOSTOLIC TEAM: The Apostolic team imparts their very life into the local church.

> So being affectionately desirous of you, we were
> willing to have imparted unto you, not the gospel of
> God only, but also our own souls, because ye were
> dear unto us.
>
> 1 Thessalonians 2:8

Impartation is one of the main goals of the apostolic team. The apostolic team will impart their very lives into the believers of the local churches. They pour out their hearts to the people. They give whatever they have willingly to the local churches. This is not just preaching or teaching, but impartation. This is what makes apostolic team ministry so powerful. The team lays down their lives for the local church.

17. THE SACRIFICE OF THE APOSTOLIC TEAM: The Apostolic team will be willing to make financial sacrifices if necessary.

> **For ye remember, brethren, our labour and travail: for labouring night and day, because we would not be chargeable unto any of you, we preached unto you the gospel of God.** 1 Thessalonians 2:9

Members of the apostolic team should be willing to make financial sacrifices if necessary to touch the nations. Some will be able to finance certain trips. God will honor these sacrifices. This will also prove that the team is not in ministry for financial gain.

18. THE CONDUCT OF THE APOSTOLIC TEAM: The Apostolic team must behave holily, and justly, and unblamely. They set an example for the local church to follow.

> **Ye are witnesses, and God also, how holily and justly and unblamably we behaved ourselves among you that believe.** 1 Thessalonians 2:10

> **For yourselves know how ye ought to follow us: for we behaved not ourselves disorderly among you.** 2 Thessalonians 3:7

The apostolic team must conduct itself in the highest standard. No one on the team must give the devil a chance to bring *reproach*. A reproach on the team is also a reproach to the sending church. Nothing must be said or done that is sinful or even appears to be evil. The team must be a model for the church they minister in. There must be no strife or division between team members.

19. THE HEART OF THE APOSTOLIC TEAM: The Apostolic team exhorts, comforts and charges the local church.

For our exhortation was not of deceit, nor of uncleanness, nor in guile.

As ye know how we exhorted and comforted and charged every one of you, as a father does his children.
1 Thessalonians 2:3,11

The apostolic team will exhort, comfort and charge the local church. To *exhort* means to call near. The team calls the church near to God. The church will experience a closer relationship to the Lord. The team does not come to draw people to themselves, but to God.

The apostolic team exhorts the church to prayer, holiness, love, worship, praise, and giving. To *comfort* means to encourage or console. This is important, especially to churches that have had trouble.

To *charge* means to scourge. The apostolic team is able to bring correction. This is based on the relationship that has formed between the two, likened to a father and his children. Correction must come out of relationship. There exists a bond of genuine love between the apostolic team and the local churches.

20. THE STANDARD OF THE APOSTOLIC TEAM: The Apostolic team influences the local church to walk worthy of God.

That ye would walk worthy of God, who hath called you unto his kingdom and glory.

1 Thessalonians 2:12

The ministry of the apostolic team will cause the church to walk worthy of God. They lift the standard of holiness and righteousness for the church. They encourage the saints to walk in love, unity, and sanctification which is well pleasing to God. The team's goal is to cause the saints to experience *kingdom living*. The kingdom of God has higher standards than the world.

21. *THE RESULTS OF THE APOSTOLIC TEAM:* The word of the Apostolic team will work effectually in the believers.

> **For this cause also thank we God without ceasing, because, when ye received the word of God which ye heard of us, ye received it not as the word of men, but as it is in truth, the word of God, which effectually worketh also in you that believe.**
>
> **1 Thessalonians 2:13**

The Word deposited into the church by the apostolic team will work effectually in the believers. The Word will continue to work even after the team has departed. The Amplified version says "exercising its (superhuman) power in those who adhere to and trust in and rely on it." The apostolic team can expect the Word deposited to work supernaturally in the church. Apostolic ministry has always been God's pattern for the church, and it brings supernatural results.

22. *THE MODEL OF THE APOSTOLIC TEAM:* The Apostolic team releases a model for the churches to follow.

> **For ye, brethren, became followers of the churches of God which in Judea are in Christ Jesus: for ye also have suffered like things of your own countrymen, even as they have of the Jews.**
>
> **1 Thessalonians 2:14**

The apostolic team is able to duplicate the model from which they are sent. Antioch churches will release a model for apostolic churches to be raised up in different nations. The team comes with blueprints that the churches can build with. The Knox translation says: *"You took for your model, brethren, the churches of God which are assembled in Judea in the name of Jesus Christ."*

23. THE RETURN OF THE APOSTOLIC TEAM: The Apostolic team should desire to return.

> But we, brethren, being taken from you for a short time in presence, not in heart, endeavored the more abundantly to see your face with great desire.
>
> 1 Thessalonians 2:17

> For God is my record, how greatly I long after you all in the bowels of Jesus Christ.
>
> Philippians 1:8

Although the team leaves physically, their heart remains with the local church. They will desire to return and be a blessing again. This is because there is a genuine bond in the spirit between the team and the local church.

24. THE OPPOSITION TO THE APOSTOLIC TEAM: Satan will often attempt to prevent the Apostolic team from returning.

> Wherefore we would have come unto you, even I Paul, once and again; but Satan hindered us.
>
> 1 Thessalonians 2:18

Satan hates and fears the visit of the apostolic team. He will do everything in his power to prevent the team from coming. He fights the relationship between the team and the local churches. This is why prayer is such an important part of apostolic ministry. Prayer helps neutralize the opposition of the enemy, and releases the plans and purposes of God for the Church.

25. THE GLORY AND JOY OF THE APOSTOLIC TEAM: The local church becomes the team's glory and joy.

> For what is our hope, or joy, or crown of rejoicing?
> Are not even ye in the presence of our Lord Jesus
> Christ at his coming?
>
> For ye are our glory and joy.
>
> > 1 Thessalonians 2:19,20
>
> Therefore, my brethren, dearly beloved and
> longed for, my joy and crown, so stand fast in the Lord,
> my dearly beloved.
> > Philippians 4:1

The team glories in the growth and health of the
local church. The church becomes the team's joy and
crown. Eternal rewards will come to the team that
invests and ties itself to local churches. The team rejoices
over the church as a father does over his son.

26. THE CONCERN OF THE APOSTOLIC TEAM: The Apostolic team will seek to further establish and comfort the
local churches.

> And sent Timotheus, our brother, and minister of
> God, and our fellow labourer in the gospel of Christ,
> to establish you, and to comfort you concerning your
> faith.
> > 1 Thessalonians 3:2

The team will seek to return for further ministry.
This is for the purpose of establishing and comforting
the churches. Paul sent Timothy to do this when he
could not come himself. Satan's attacks on church plants
and local churches are countered by the visit of the apostolic team.

27. THE FOLLOW UP OF THE APOSTOLIC TEAM: The
Apostolic team will follow up on the condition of the
local churches.

> For this cause, when I could no longer forbear, I sent to know your faith, lest by some means the tempter have tempted you, and our labour be in vain.
>
> **1 Thessalonians 3:5**

> But I trust in the Lord Jesus to send Timotheus shortly unto you, that I also may be of good comfort, when I know your state.
>
> **Philippians 2:19**

The team checks up on the condition of the local churches. This is important because we don't want our labor to be in vain. The team is always aware of Satan's attempt to destroy the work of God. The team monitors the condition of the churches they minister in.

28. *The life of the Apostolic team:* The Apostolic team's life becomes connected to the churches they minister in.

> **For now we live, if ye stand fast in the Lord.**
>
> **1 Thessalonians 3:8**

This is a powerful verse of scripture. Paul is basing his very life on the health of the church. I am reminded the words of Judah concerning the relationship between Jacob and Benjamin: *"...seeing that his life is bound up in the lad's life."* The apostle's life is tied to the church. The team becomes one with the churches they minister in. Their very life is dependent upon the growth and health of the church.

29. *The goal of the Apostolic team:* The apostolic team perfects that which is lacking in the faith of the saints.

> **Night and day praying exceedingly that we might see your face, that we might perfect that which is lacking in your faith?**
>
> **1 Thessalonians 3:10**

The apostolic team does not come to duplicate what the local leadership has already accomplished. They come to perfect the areas of lack in the church. To *perfect* means to complete. Local churches can lack in the areas of praise and worship, deliverance, prophecy, prayer, prosperity, love, faith, and evangelism. The team can identify the areas of lack and minister in these areas. The apostolic team will help perfect the saints (Ephesians 4).

30. THE LOVE OF THE APOSTOLIC TEAM: The Apostolic team's love continues to increase toward the local churches.

> **And the Lord make you to increase and abound in love one toward another, and toward all men, even as we do toward you.**
> **1 Thessalonians 3:12**

The team's love for the local church continues to grow in time. The relationship becomes stronger. Strong relationships are forged between the team and the local church. This opens the way for even more trust and impartation. The greater the love for the church, the more effective the ministry.

31. THE REVELATION OF THE APOSTOLIC TEAM: The Apostolic team brings an understanding of the mysteries of God to the local church.

> **Let a man so account of us, as the ministers of Christ, and stewards of the mysteries of God.**
> **1 Corinthians 4:1**

The apostolic team releases revelation to the local churches. The teams act as stewards of the mysteries of God. As churches receive the apostolic team, they will increase in wisdom, knowledge and understanding. It is given unto us to know the mysteries of the kingdom (Matthew 13). Apostles are sent to preach the kingdom of heaven (Matthew 10).

Churches that receive the apostolic team will be upgraded in current truth and revelation. Releasing revelation is a major function of apostolic ministry (Ephesians 3).

32. *THE REPORT OF THE APOSTOLIC TEAM:* The Apostolic team reports back to the church from where they were sent.

And thence they sailed to Antioch, from whence they had been recommended to the grace of God for the work which they fulfilled.

And when they were come, and had gathered the church together, they rehearsed all that God had done with them, and how he had opened the door of faith unto the Gentiles.

Acts 14:26,27

This is an encouragement to the sending church. The team is the extension of the sending church. There is a spiritual connection between the two. Both work together to advance the Kingdom of God. After the fulfillment of the task, the apostolic team returns to the local church until they leave again. They may be sent out for new endeavors or simply desire to return to the churches they helped or established.

The apostolic team must honor and respect the presbytery of a local church. They must never undermine the authority of the local presbytery. The local presbytery must receive and honor the input of the apostolic team if they desire to be blessed through its ministry.

"The apostolic teams can help open new areas in the spirit dimension for prayer, warfare, worship or the operation of the gifts. These new avenues of ministry will release fresh spirit measure into the lives of the believers and drastically affect the spiritual atmosphere over the local church. The apostolic team can release new revelation of truth, prophetic insight, and the operation of the

gifts for miracles and healings. This will add to the local work an inheritance of spirit momentum and power. The visit of the apostolic team refreshes, revitalizes and repositions the local churches for more effective ministry."

Apostolic Strategies
Jonathan David

33. *THE INTERCESSION OF THE APOSTOLIC TEAM:* The Apostolic teams continue to pray for the local churches.

PAUL, and Silvanus, and Timotheus, unto the church of the Thessalonians which is in God the Father and in the Lord Jesus Christ: Grace be unto you, and peace, from God our Father, and the Lord Jesus Christ.

We give thanks to God always for you all, making mention of you in our prayers;

Remembering without ceasing your work of faith, and labour of love, and patience of hope in our Lord Jesus Christ, in the sight of God and our Father;

Knowing, brethren beloved, your election of God.

1 Thessalonians 1:1-4

I thank my God upon every remembrance of you,

Always in every prayer of mine for you all making request with joy,

Philippians 1:3,4

There is a bonding between the apostolic team and the local churches they minister in. The apostolic team will remember the church and pray for them. The relationship between the apostolic team and the local church is not casual. There will be a strong covenant bond between the two. These bonds are based on genuine love.

Intercession is a major part of apostolic ministry. Apostolic praying helps release local churches into new realms of glory and power.

34. *THE NEED OF THE APOSTOLIC TEAM:* The local churches should be encouraged to pray for the Apostolic team. The team needs the prayers of the churches.

Brethren, pray for us.

1 Thessalonians 5:25

Finally, brethren pray for us, that the word of the Lord may have free course, and be glorified, even as it is with you.

2 Thessalonians 3:1

The local churches should also pray for the apostolic team. This will open new doors for the team to minister in other regions. The team is strengthened by the prayers of the local churches they minister in. There is a mutual relationship, with each group praying for the other.

35. *THE RESPECT OF THE APOSTOLIC TEAM:* The apostolic team honors and respects leadership. The team will build up the membership of the local church. They will do nothing to demean or lower the leadership in the eyes of the people. They will encourage the saints to esteem the leadership highly.

And we beseech you, brethren, to know them which labour among you, and are over you in the LORD, and admonish you;

And to esteem them very highly in love for their work's sake.

1 Thessalonians 5:12,13

36. *THE ENCOURAGEMENT OF THE APOSTOLIC TEAM:* The apostolic team encourages the manifestation of the Holy Spirit.

Quench not the Spirit.

Despise not prophesyings.

Prove all things; hold fast that which is good.

1 Thessalonians 5:19-21

The Conybeare translation says, *"Quench not* [the manifestation] *of the Spirit."* Spiritual gifts are important in the local church, and they should be encouraged. The apostolic team will help stir up these manifestations. This is especially true concerning prophecy. The Knox translation says, *"Do not stifle the utterances of the Spirit."* The NEB says, *"Do not stifle inspiration."*

The apostolic team will place honor on the gift of prophecy. The Knox translation says, *"Do not hold prophecy in low esteem."* Prophecy is to be highly regarded in the Church. There is a danger in believers despising prophesy. We are told to despise not prophesy. It is an important gift that edifies and builds up the local assembly. These manifestations will profit the Church (1 Corinthians 12:7).

The Samuel Principle

Samuel is a type of apostolic ministry. His ministry released a fresh wave of the prophetic anointing in Israel. He trained prophets and established a school of prophets. Samuel maintained a circuit of ministry.

And he went from year to year in circuit to Bethel, and Gilgal, and Mizpeh, and judged Israel in all those places.

1 Samuel 7:16

Samuel established a network for his ministry. Apostolic networks are being birthed around the globe. Apostolic teams are vital to the strength of these networks. Teams can visit the churches in the network and

41

continually upgrade and impart fresh anointing to the network churches. There is also a cross pollination as different networks relate and draw from one another's strengths.

In addition to planting new churches, the apostolic team can visit and strengthen existing churches . They can develop a circuit of ministry as Samuel did. This can be done on a yearly basis, or by invitation from the churches at certain times. There will also be certain nations that the team will visit on a regular basis, in addition to new ones.

Chapter 3
Apostles and Prophets: Builders in the Spirit

"A strong team is made up of forceful, mature, proven ministries. In particular, a senior apostle will always make a special place for a godly, gifted prophet, and will want him alongside himself as an indispensable pivotal hub around which all the other gifts revolve" (pg. 211).

Apostles Today,
Barney Coombs

Apostles and prophets are linked together more than any other two gifts in the New Testament. Apostolic teams can include all five-fold ministers, but it is important to have apostles and prophets working together. They are the two highest ranking gifts, and both carry tremendous authority in the spirit realm (1 Corinthians 12:28).

Apostles and prophets are the power officers of the Church. Power is defined as the ability to do or act. It is the capability of doing or accomplishing something. An officer is one who holds a position of rank or authority in an organization. Power is also defined as great or marked ability to do or act. It means strength, might, force, or authority. A *power officer* is a person who holds a position of rank with the power and authority to accomplish something. Apostles and prophets are necessary to execute the purposes of God.

Since apostles and prophets carry the highest spiritual rank in the church, they both have authority as sent ones to root out, pull down, destroy, throw down, build, and plant (Jeremiah 1:10).

And are built upon the foundation of the apostles and prophets, Jesus Christ himself being the chief corner stone.

Ephesians 2:20

Apostles and prophets lay foundation. They deal with the belief systems that people build their lives upon. They challenge false belief systems and mindsets that are contrary to the word of God.

Zerubbabel, Ezra, Haggai, Zechariah: Old Testament Types

These four men represent apostles and prophets working together to build the temple of the Lord. Zerubbabel is a type of the apostle in that he laid the foundation of the temple.

The hands of Zerubbabel have laid the foundation of this house; his hands shall also finish it; and thou shalt know that the LORD of hosts hath sent me unto you.

Zechariah 4:9

Zechariah was sent to Zerubbabel to encourage him through prophecy. Both Haggai and Zechariah prophesied to the Jews concerning the rebuilding of the temple. They stirred the people to work through prophecy. They helped the people overcome impossible odds in restoring the temple.

Then the prophets, Haggai the prophet, and Zechariah the son of Iddo, prophesied unto the Jews

that were in Judah and Jerusalem in the name of the
God of Israel, even unto them.

Then rose up Zerubbabel the son of Shealtiel, and
Jeshua the son of Jozadak, and began to build the
house of God which is at Jerusalem: and with them
were the prophets of God helping them.

Ezra 5:1,2

Ezra is also a type of apostolic ministry. He was
sent by the king to teach the law of the Lord.

Forasmuch as thou art sent of the king, and his
seven counsellors, to enquire concerning Judah and
Jerusalem, according to the law of thy God which is in
thine hand.

Ezra 7:14

Ezra worked alongside Zerubbabel, Haggai, and
Zechariah. He was a scribe who taught the people the
law of the Lord.

The Jews prospered through the prophesying of
Haggai and Zechariah. Likewise, local churches will
prosper through the prophesying of the apostolic
team.

Zerubbabel, Ezra, and Zechariah are an example of
a team working together to build the house of the Lord.
The temple was built in spite of intense opposition.

Which in other ages was not made known unto the
sons of men, as it is now revealed unto his holy apostles and prophets by the Spirit.

Ephesians 3:5

Apostles and prophets bring revelation to the
church. They are stewards of the mysteries of God.
They release to the church an understanding of the
plans and purposes of God. They bring a revelation
to the church of secrets hidden in previous ages.

45

> **Rejoice over her, thou heaven, and ye holy apostles and prophets; for God hath avenged you on her.**
>
> **Revelation 18:20**

Apostles and prophets are hated by Babylon. They expose false teaching, heresy, and wickedness. They expose the lies and deception of Babylon. They bring deliverance to churches causing them to walk in the liberty of the Holy Spirit.

Apostles and prophets should be a part of the apostolic team. These two ministries are breakthrough ministries that help local churches breakthrough into new realms of Spirit life. The preaching, teaching, and prophesying of the apostolic team will release fresh revelation and new moves of the Holy Spirit into the local church.

The Apostolic Team, especially apostles and prophets are important for churches in transition. Graham Cooke states,

> *"In transition we will need friends from outside who can provide objective support and care. We also need access to people who understand transition and process. In transition, we are redigging the foundation of the church so that the lord can erect a bigger building and release a greater dynamic of corporate power and identity. The only people who can really help us now are apostles and prophets. They are foundation ministers.*
>
> *It is inevitable in transition that our structures are going to change. New paradigms need to form as God delivers us from being a stereotype to a prototype church. Changes must come. We need prophetic insight and apostolic strategy combining together to redevelop the foundation and structure of the work.*

Apostles and prophets together are the eye in the storm, bringing peace and order into chaos. They are a catalyst to provide breakthrough. By teaching, advice, prophecy, and impartation, they can furnish the building blocks to enable us to bridge the gap between where we are now and where we aspire to be.

The combined resources of apostle and prophet will bring us to the place in God where there is a release in the Spirit realm" (pp. 352-353).

A Divine Confrontation
Graham Cooke

Prophecy is especially important to release individuals and churches into their destinies. Corporate prophecy and personal prophecy gives direction and activates believers to enter fully into the plan of God.

The laying on of hands for impartation is also important. The apostolic team will release a measure of Holy Spirit life into a local church. They will increase the level of anointing in the local church.

Prophets have a grace to discern particular strongholds over a church or a region. They have keen insight into what a church or region needs. This is why they are so vital to the success of a team. Prophets also have an anointing in intercession. They can preach and teach prophetically, releasing revelation that is critical for a particular area.

The prophet's words carry power to breakthrough, pull down, and ignite. These ministries release LIFE (John 6:63). Many prophets carry a revival anointing that can initiate revival in a church or region. Prophets can also help identify the giftings in a church for activation and release.

Apostolic Decrees and Prophetic Declarations

Apostolic decrees and prophetic declarations need to be uttered in every territory and region of the earth. These are proclamations uttered through apostolic teams that release and establish God's plans and purposes for each nation. A *decree* is an authoritative command given by governmental officers. Apostles and prophets are governmental officers of the church (1 Corinthians 12:28). These proclamations are prophetic in nature and apostolic in origin. They originate from the apostolic mandate to see the kingdom of God established in every nation. Decrees are tools that help us see the fulfillment of the Great Commission.

> **Now in the first year of Cyrus, king of Persia, that the word of the LORD by the mouth of Jeremiah might be fulfilled, the LORD stirred up the spirit of Cyrus king of Persia, that he made a PROCLAMATION throughout all his kingdom...**
>
> **Ezra 1:1**

The Lord stirs up His servants to issue these DECREES. These decrees mobilize the people to rise up and do the will of God (Ezra 1:5). Decrees mobilize leaders and families. Issuing decrees will mobilize the leaders in the nations and families of the earth (Ezra 2). Decrees release the resources necessary for the accomplishment of the purposes of God (Ezra 2:69).

Apostolic teams will go into different regions and issue prophetic declarations to extend the kingdom of God. The apostles and prophets will speak authoritatively to the principalities and powers of a region to cause breakthrough and release. This is why it is important to have members of the team who know how to speak prophetically over nations and kingdoms (Jeremiah 1:9,10). The apostolic team is able to root out, pull down, destroy, throw down, build, and plant. They are sent ones with authority to speak on the behalf of heaven.

Apostolic Impartation
(Romans 1:11)

One of the major functions of the ministry of the apostle and the apostolic team is to impart grace and anointing to those who receive the ministry. This truth is seen throughout the Bible. Apostles have the ability to release others into new measures of Spirit life. This is done through laying on of hands, prophecy, or association.

To *impart* means to share or grant a part of. Impartation is the ability to transfer gifts and grace from one person to another. The anointing can be transferred. The apostle and the apostolic team shares its grace and life with those to whom they minister. Paul desired to see the church at Rome in order to impart unto them some spiritual gift (Romans 1:11). This is the desire of apostolic ministry. We find the law of impartation operating throughout the word of God.

Moses

Moses is a type of the apostle. He was SENT by God into Egypt (Exodus 3:10). The definition of *apostle* is A SENT ONE. He was sent into Egypt with signs and wonders to deliver Israel. Apostles operate with signs and wonders and also bring deliverance.

> **And the Lord said unto Moses, Gather unto me seventy men of the elders of Israel, whom thou knowest to be the elders of the people, and officers over them; and bring them unto the tabernacle of the congregation, that they may stand there with thee.**

And I will come down and talk with thee there: and I will take of the spirit which is upon thee, and will put it upon them; and they shall bear the burden of the people with thee, that thou bear it not thyself alone.

Numbers 11:16,17

And the Lord came down in a cloud, and spake unto him, and took of the spirit that was upon him, and gave it unto the seventy elders: and it came to pass, that, when the spirit rested upon them, they PROPHESIED, and did not cease.

But there remained two of the men in the camp, the name of the one was Eldad, and the name of the other Medad: and the spirit rested upon them; and they were of them that were written, but went not out unto the tabernacle: and they prophesied in the camp.

And there ran a young man, and told Moses, and said, Eldad and Medad do prophesy in the camp.

And Joshua the son of Nun, the servant of Moses, one of his young men, answered and said, My lord Moses, forbid them.

And Moses said unto him, Enviest thou for my sake? would God that all the Lord's people were prophets, and that the Lord would put his spirit upon them!

Numbers 11:25-29

When the spirit that was upon Moses rested on the seventy, they prophesied. There was an impartation that took place. To *impart* means to share. God shared the anointing that was upon Moses with the seventy. They were released into a prophetic realm. The apostolic ministry has the grace to release others into new spiritual realms.

The seventy elders were leaders in Israel. They were chosen because of their maturity and wisdom.

50

Leaders should operate in a prophetic dimension. When Joshua asked Moses to stop the two elders that were outside the camp, Moses replied, "I wish that all the Lord's people were prophets, and that the Lord would put His spirit upon them."

The desire of an apostle should be to see all of God's people partake of the anointing. Apostles desire to share the grace in their lives with the people of God. They have a desire to impart and release the anointing into the lives of the saints in order for them to operate in the Spirit. The seventy elders began to operate in a realm they had never operated in before. They had the same ability to prophesy as Moses did.

> **And the Lord said unto Moses, Take thee Joshua the son of Nun, a man in whom is the spirit, and lay thine hand upon him;**
>
> **And set him before Eleazar the priest, and before all the congregation; and give him a charge in their sight.**
>
> **And thou shalt put some of thine honour upon him, that all the congregation of the children of Israel may be obedient.**
>
> **Numbers 27:18-20**

Moses was commanded by God to put some of his honor upon Joshua. He was to share a portion of his honor with Joshua. As noted before, to "impart" means to give or share.

The word *honor* refers to glory, power, strength, might or greatness. Apostles have the grace and ability to release honor upon those whom God sends them to.

> **And Joshua the son of Nun was full of the spirit of wisdom; for Moses had laid his hands upon him: and**

the children of Israel hearkened unto him, and did as the Lord commanded Moses.

Deuteronomy 34:9

Joshua received the spirit of wisdom through the laying on of hands. This caused the people to listen to Joshua. They recognized the same spirit upon Joshua that was upon Moses. Moses was able to share a part of his spirit through the laying on of hands.

Samuel

Samuel is the next person we will look at as an example of apostolic impartation. Samuel is also a type of the apostle. He was a prophet and priest who judged Israel. The judges were all types of the apostolic ministry. They brought deliverance and judged. The spirit of judgment operates through an apostle. Moses brought the judgments of God into Egypt and delivered Israel. Whenever there is deliverance, there will also be judgment.

Samuel was sent by the Lord to anoint both Saul and David. Apostles have the grace and ability to release the anointing into the lives of those to whom they are sent.

Then Samuel took a vial of oil, and poured it upon his head, and kissed him, and said, "Is it not because the Lord hath anointed thee to be captain over his inheritance?"

After that thou shalt come to the hill of God, where is the garrison of the Philistines: and it shall come to pass, when thou art come thither to the city, that thou shalt meet a company of prophets coming down from the high place with a psaltery, and a tabret, and a pipe, and a harp, before them; and they shall prophesy:

> And the Spirit of the Lord will come upon thee, and thou shalt prophesy with them, and shalt be turned into another man.
>
> And it was so, that when he had turned his back to go from Samuel, God gave him another heart: and all those signs came to pass that day.
>
> And when they came thither to the hill, behold, a company of prophets met him; and the Spirit of God came upon him, and he prophesied among them.
>
> 1 Samuel 10:1,5,6,9,10

Samuel anoints Saul and directs him to a company of prophets. Saul comes into contact with the prophets and begins to prophesy. All of this was initiated by coming into contact with Samuel. Saul begins to operate in a new spiritual realm. He had never prophesied before being anointed. One day he was looking for his father's lost donkeys, and the next day he is prophesying.

Samuel also anointed David to be king after the rejection of Saul.

> Then Samuel took the horn of oil, and anointed him in the midst of his brethren: and the Spirit of the Lord came upon David from that day forward. So Samuel rose up, and went to Ramah.
>
> 1 Samuel 16:13

The Spirit of the Lord came upon David from the moment he was anointed by Samuel. Samuel was sent to David to anoint him and release him into the flow of the Spirit. Apostles are sent to release people into the flow of the Holy Spirit. This is the power of impartation.

> And Saul sent messengers to take David: and when they saw the company of the prophets prophesying, and Samuel standing as appointed over them, the

> Spirit of God was upon the messengers of Saul, and they also prophesied.
>
> 1 Samuel 19:20

Samuel was appointed by God to stand over the prophets. He provided a place for prophets to be trained and released into the prophetic realm. These prophets had received an impartation from Samuel. Apostles have the ability to impart and release prophets into their ministries. Prophets are seldom released by pastors or administrators. It takes apostles or prophets to impart and release prophets into their ministries.

Apostolic churches provide an atmosphere for the moving of the Holy Spirit. This is typified by *Ramah* which means height, or a high place. Ramah is a place conducive for operating in higher realms of the Spirit. The anointing was so strong in Ramah that the messengers of Saul began to prophesy when they came into the atmosphere. They became partakers of the anointing and grace that flowed from Samuel at Ramah.

David

"These be the names of the mighty men who David had..." (2 Samuel 23:8). The twenty-third chapter of Samuel gives a list of David's mighty men. They include Adino the Eznite, Eleazar the Ahonite, and Shammah the Haraite. These men were partakers of the anointing upon David's life. David was able to impart a measure of his spirit into these fighting men. **The apostolic anointing is a warring anointing.** Apostles release a spirit of might to the saints. David's mighty men are another example of the power of impartation.

Elijah

Elijah was one of Israel's greatest prophets. He is also a type of the apostolic. He was sent to anoint two kings and a prophet.

54

> And the LORD said unto him, Go, return on thy
> way to the wilderness of Damascus: and when thou
> comest, anoint Hazael to be king over Syria:
>
> And Jehu the son of Nimshi shalt thou anoint to
> be king over Israel: and Elisha the son is Shaphat of
> Abel-meholah shalt thou anoint to be prophet in thy
> room.
>
> **1 Kings 19:15,16**

Elijah anointed Hazael who executed judgment
against Israel. He anointed Jehu who executed judgment against Jezebel and the house of Ahab. He
anointed Elisha to be prophet in his place.

Elijah was also over the school of the prophets.
He carried a similar anointing and grace as Samuel.
He was able to impart to those under his care and
authority. By anointing kings he released them into a
new realm of authority. This is a function of the apostle — *to release others into higher realms of authority.*
They receive the anointing and authority to execute
judgment.

> And when the sons of the prophets which were to
> view at Jericho saw him, they said, The spirit of Elijah
> doth rest on Elisha....
>
> **2 Kings 2:15**

Elisha received a double portion of Elijah's spirit.
This was the portion of the firstborn. Elisha was able
to operate in a greater level than Elijah. Elisha shared
Elijah's anointing. This is the law of impartation.

Jesus Imparts the
Holy Spirit to the Disciples

> Then said Jesus to them again, Peace be unto you:
> as my Father hath SENT me, even so SEND I you.

And when he had said this, HE BREATHED on them, and saith unto them, RECEIVE YE THE HOLY GHOST.

John 20:21,22

Jesus released the Holy Spirit to his disciples by breathing upon them. Although they were not completely filled until the day of Pentecost, they received an impartation at this time. Jesus is the Apostle of our Confession (Hebrews 3:1). He is the perfect example of a SENT ONE. He imparts to His disciples as He sends them. This is a major function of the apostolic ministry — to impart the Holy Spirit.

Peter and John

After Philip preaches the gospel in Samaria, many respond and are baptized. The apostles which were at Jerusalem send Peter and John to impart the Holy Spirit.

Now when the apostles which were at Jerusalem heard that Samaria had received the word of God, they sent unto them Peter and John:

Who, when they were come down, prayed for them, that they might receive the Holy Ghost:

(For as yet he was fallen upon none of them: only they were baptized in the name of the Lord Jesus.)

Then laid they their hands on them, and they received the Holy Ghost. And when Simon saw that through laying on of the apostles' hands the Holy Ghost was given, he offered them money,

Saying, Give me also this power, that on whomsoever I lay hands, he may receive the Holy Ghost.

Acts 8:14-19

Philip the evangelist was able to get the Samaritans into salvation, but the apostles were able to get them flowing in the Holy Spirit. They released the new believers into the baptism of the Holy Spirit through the laying on of hands. Simon tries to buy this ability and is rebuked by Peter. Simon was not trying to buy the Holy Spirit. He was trying to buy the ability to impart through the laying on of hands.

Apostles have an ability to release the saints into new dimensions of the Holy Spirit. They are sent by God to help believers move in the gifts of the Holy Spirit. This can be done by prophecy, the laying on of hands, or association.

This can also take place through preaching. As apostles preach and teach, there is a release of the anointing that comes upon those who hear. This can be seen through Peter's ministry in the household of Cornelius.

> **While Peter yet spake these words, the Holy Ghost fell on all them which heard the word.**
>
> **And they of the circumcision were astonished, as many as came with Peter, because that on the Gentiles also was poured out the gift of the Holy Ghost.**
>
> **For they heard them speak with tongues, and magnify God....**
>
> **Acts 10:44-46**

The Holy Spirit came upon them as Peter spake. There was no altar call for salvation. Those who heard the word evidently believed in their heart the message that Peter was speaking and were saved. The apostle has an anointing to release people into the fullness of the Holy Spirit. Even while Peter was giving an evangelistic message, his gifting as an apostle caused the hearers to be filled with the Holy Spirit.

Paul

And it came to pass, that, while Apollos was a Corinth, Paul having passed through the upper coasts came to Ephesus; and finding certain disciples,

He said to them, Have ye received the Holy Ghost since ye believed? And they said unto him, We have not so much as heard whether there be any Holy Ghost.

And he said unto them, Unto what then were ye baptized? And they said, Unto John's baptism.

Then said Paul, John verily baptized with the baptism of repentance, saying unto the people, that they should believe on him which should come after him, that is, on Christ Jesus.

When they heard this, they were baptized in the name of the Lord Jesus.

And when Paul had laid his hands upon them, the Holy Ghost came on them; and they spake with tongues, and prophesied.

Acts 19:1-6

Paul wants to know whether these believers have received the Holy Spirit. He finds out that they are in need of salvation, having only received John's message of the coming Messiah. He tells them the Messiah John talked about is Jesus, and baptizes them. He then lays hands on them to receive the Holy Spirit. They receive the Holy Spirit and speak in tongues and prophesy.

This is another example of the way an apostle thinks. He desires to see people moving in the things of the Holy Spirit. He locates where people are in their relation to the Holy Spirit and releases them into the area where they are lacking. This does not mean that apostles don't preach salvation. They can do the work of an evangelist (2 Timothy 4:5). Their primary motivation, however, is to get people moving beyond salvation into the fullness of the Holy Spirit. Apostles have an ability to release people through the laying on of hands.

Neglect not the gift that is in thee, which was given thee by prophecy, with the laying on of the hands of the presbytery.

1 Timothy 4:14

Timothy received a gift through prophecy and the laying on of the hands of the presbytery. Paul is telling him not to neglect the gift. Paul knew that Timothy had received through impartation. He knew the law of impartation and operated in it.

Paul knew that if Timothy did not operate in the gift, it would be due to neglect. He knew Timothy had received something when he was ordained. The early church knew how to release the gifts of God through laying on of hands and prophecy. This is what God is restoring to the Church today. He is releasing the apostolic anointing to get His people moving strongly in the things of the Holy Spirit. Ministers who are exposed to true apostles will receive gifts and anointings through impartation. Believers will move in the things of the Holy Spirit through impartation.

Whereunto I put thee in remembrance that thou stir up the gift of God, which is in thee by the putting on of my hands.

2 Timothy 1:6

Paul had laid his hands upon Timothy and imparted a gift. It was Timothy's responsibility to stir up that gift. Paul knew Timothy had received the gift through his hands. Paul was functioning in his apostolic gifting to release Timothy into the fullness of the Holy Spirit.

Apostles and apostolic teams have a ministry of impartation. They help release churches and believers into new dimensions of the Spirit. Apostolic teams are powerful groups of five-fold ministers who labor to help build local churches. They understand that a strong local church will impact their communities and nations. The gates of hell cannot prevail against the church that is built apostolically.

The apostolic ministry is anointed by the Lord to increase the level of power and revelation of the local churches. Pastors would be wise to connect with an Antioch church that releases teams. The apostolic team does what the local leadership is unable to do. They come to release the purposes of God for the local church. Apostles and apostolic teams will be strategic ministries for entire regions and nations. God is once again restoring the function of apostles and apostolic teams. We are seeing breakthroughs in many territories as a result of the release of apostolic teams. We are praying for the formation and release of thousands of these teams to impact the world.

Different Methods of Impartation

1. By Words

(John 6:63). Words carry spiritual power. They can be containers of the anointing. This includes PROPHECY (1 Samuel 10:5,6), PREACHING (Acts 10:44), TEACHING (Deuteronomy 32:3), and CONVERSING (Luke 24:32).

2. By Association

A person can receive an impartation by being a part of an apostolic and prophetic company. You are affected by the people you associate with. Saul was turned into another man when he came into contact with the company of prophets (1 Samuel 10:5,6).

3. By Tangible Objects or Physical Contact

This can include ANOINTING OIL (1 Samuel 16:13), LAYING ON OF HANDS (Deuteronomy 34:9), PRAYER CLOTHS (Acts 19:12), and BLOWING BREATH (John 20:22).

The apostolic team can use these various methods to impart a fresh spirit measure into the churches. These churches will be changed and come into a higher spiritual frequency as a result of impartation. There is a real spirit measure released through the apostolic team. It is tangible. Impartation does not result from empty, religious, or ceremonial rituals. There are real transfers of power through the apostolic team.

> And my speech and my preaching was not with enticing words of man's wisdom, but in DEMON-STRATION of the Spirit and of power.
>
> 1 Corinthians 2:4

> And as ye go, preach, saying, The kingdom of heaven is at hand.
>
> Heal the sick, cleanse the lepers, raise the dead, cast out devils: freely ye have received, freely give.
>
> Matthew 10:7,8

Apostolic ministry is a ministry of DEMONSTRA-TION. Apostles and apostolic teams visibly DEMON-STRATE the kingdom of God. Remember the kingdom of God is not in word but in POWER (1 Corinthians 4:20). Miracles, signs and wonders are a necessary part of this ministry. The apostolic team models the kingdom of God. The apostles were sent to preach, heal the sick, cleanse the lepers, cast out devils, and raise the dead. People need to see the DEMON-STRATION of the kingdom. The Williams translation says, "they were attended with proof and power given by the Spirit." People need PROOF that our message is from God.

> **Through mighty signs and wonders, by the power of the spirit of God; so that from Jerusalem, and round about unto Illyricum, I have fully preached the gospel of Christ.**
> **Romans 15:19**

The gospel is fully preached when it is accompanied by signs and wonders. The apostolic team brings a message with signs and wonders. This will cause breakthrough into new regions and territories. This is the PIONEERING aspect of the Apostolic Team. They are sent with power and authority to DEMONSTRATE THE KINGDOM OF GOD. As the apostolic team travels, they should expect to see signs and wonders.

As the Church understands and develops strong presbyteries and apostolic teams, their line will be extended throughout the earth. I believe the fulfillment of the Great Commission is dependent upon the Church's obedience in this area. The Holy Spirit is mobilizing the Church to FINISH THE JOB. May we respond to the Holy Spirit's leading and be the generation that brings back the KING.

As local churches develop presbyteries and apostolic teams, they will experience breakthroughs into regions and territories. There will be an expansion of the kingdom of God throughout the earth. What I have shared is the pattern for the New Testament, *apostolic ministry*. These are strategies that will cause success in fulfilling the Great Commission. May God's blessing be upon those who rise up and build according to God's blueprint found in the Word of God.

References

1. *Apostolic Strategies Affecting Nations*, by Jonathan David (1997), self-published.

2. *The Complete Wineskin*, by Harold Eberle (1993), Winepress Publishing, Yakima, WA.

3. *The Last Apostles On Earth*, by Roger Sapp (1995), Companion Press, Shippensburg, PA.

4. *Apostolic Teams* Tape Series by Derek Prince, Derek Prince Ministries, Ft. Lauderdale, FL.

5. *Apostles and Shepherds* Tape Series by Derek Prince, Derek Prince Ministries, Ft. Lauderdale, FL.

6. *Apostles Today* by Barney Coombs (1996), Sovereign World Ltd., Kent, England.

7. *The Normal Christian Church Life* by Watchman Nee (1980), Living Stream Ministry, Anaheim, CA.

8. *A Divine Confrontation* by Graham Cooke (1999), Destiny Image, Shippensburg, PA.

Other books by John Eckhardt

To order books and tapes contact:

Crusaders I.M.P.A.C.T.
P.O. Box 492
Matteson, IL 60443
(708) 922-0983

For ministry engagements contact:

Crusaders Ministries
P.O. Box 7211
Chicago, IL 60680
(773) 637-2121